STEVE JOBS
AND THE STORY OF APPLE

Fiona Beddall

LEVEL 3

SCHOLASTIC

Written by: Fiona Beddall

Publisher: Jacquie Bloese

Editor: Fiona Davis

Designer: Mo Choy

Picture research: Emma Bree

Photo credits:

Cover: P. Sakuma/PA. **Pages 4 & 5:** DB Apple/DPA, L. Psihoyos, N. Feanny Hicks/Corbis; Polaris/Eyevine; Apple/DPA/PA; A. Wyman/Getty Images; Courtesy of Apple; crossroadscreative, J. Doiy/iStockphoto. **Page 6:** D. P. Morris/Getty Images. **Page 9:** Polaris/Eyevine. **Page 11:** Computer History Museum. **Page 13:** Dorling Kindersley/Alamy. **Page 15:** R. Bremec/iStockphoto. **Page 17:** Science and Society Picture Library/Getty Images; B. Thissen/Corbis. **Pages 20 & 21:** T. Munnecke, Science and Society Picture Library/Getty Images. **Page 24:** T. Thai/Polaris/Eyevine. **Page 27:** E. Kashi/Corbis. **Page 29:** AP/PA. **Page 31:** A. Etra/Time Life/Getty Images. **Page 32:** E. Kashi/Corbis. **Pages 34 & 35:** D. Walker/SJ/Contour/Getty Images; E. Kashi/VII/Corbis. **Page 37:** Disney/Pixar; Allstar. **Pages 40 & 41:** Advertising Archives; S. Ragan/AP/PA. **Page 42 & 43:** Apple Corp/Getty Images. **Page 44:** J. Sullivan/Getty Images. **Page 46:** T. Mosenfelder/Getty Images. **Page 48:** J. Sullivan/Getty Images; Courtesy of Apple. **Page 51:** Courtesy of Apple. **Pages 52 & 53:** L. Suzuki/San Francisco Chronicle/Corbis; J. Sullivan/Getty Images. **Pages 54 & 55:** J. Sullivan, K. Djansezian/ Getty Images. **Pages 56 & 57:** Interfoto, J. Henshall/Alamy; Bettmann/Corbis: Luzanin, M. Kurtz, Avelasevic/iStockphoto; Cake/Sony. **Pages 58 & 59:** F. Bimmer/Corbis: T. Yamanaka/AFP, J. Sullivan/Getty Images; K. Nawrocki/iStockphoto. **Pages 60 & 61:** Ming H2 Wu/Blend/Corbis; R. Bingham/Alamy; E. Gutenberger/iStockphoto; Facebook; Twitter.

Published by Scholastic Ltd. 2012

Printed in Singapore

Reprinted in 2013

Contents

	Page
Steve Jobs and the story of Apple	**4–55**
People and places	**4**
Introduction	**6**
Chapter 1: Crazy about electronics	**7**
Chapter 2: The birth of Apple	**13**
Chapter 3: A computer in colour	**19**
Chapter 4: The first Mac	**25**
Chapter 5: Starting again	**30**
Chapter 6: A family man	**34**
Chapter 7: 'Think different!'	**38**
Chapter 8: '1000 songs in your pocket'	**43**
Chapter 9: A phone for the 21st century	**47**
Chapter 10: Designing the future	**50**
Remembering Steve	**54**
Fact Files	**56–61**
Inventions that changed our world	**56**
Entrepreneurs of the digital age	**58**
How to be an entrepreneur	**60**
Self-Study Activities	**62–64**
New Words	**inside back cover**

STEVE JOBS

Steve Jobs in 1971, at the age of 16.

Steve with Woz (Steve Wozniak). Together, they started Apple in 1976.

Silicon Valley's most famous entrepreneur in 1995.

Steve's sister, writer Mona Simpson, who he first met in 1986.

Steve in 2010 with his wife, Laurene Powell.

PLACES

The garage in Los Altos, California, where Steve and Woz worked on the first Apple computer.

One of over 350 Apple Stores in the world today.

The Santa Clara Valley (or Silicon Valley) in California. It's the home of many famous companies, including Apple, Google, eBay, Intel and Facebook. There are more millionaires there than in any other part of the USA.

SAN FRANCISCO BAY

CALIFORNIA

PACIFIC OCEAN

Silicon Valley •

STEVE JOBS
AND THE STORY OF APPLE

INTRODUCTION

In 1976, two young friends, Steve Jobs and Steve Wozniak, started a computer company in a garage in California, USA. They called the company Apple and their dream was for computers to be a part of everyone's lives.

Forty years later, their dream has come true. Apple employs 60,000 people and has 357 shops around the world. Customers spend more than $100 billion a year on its computers, mobile phones and music players. In August 2011, it became the world's largest company.

Together with Apple, Steve Jobs brought huge changes to many industries, including computers, music, mobile phones and books. Hundreds of millions of people around the world use the technology that he helped to create – technology which changed the face of the modern world.

CHAPTER 1
Crazy about electronics

'When I was a kid, my dad made me believe that I could build anything.'
Steve Jobs

Joanne Schieble was an American student, and she was in love with a teaching assistant at her university. His name was Abdulfattah Jandali. The two twenty-three-year-olds had spent a wonderful summer with Abdulfattah's family in Syria, but now they were back in the USA and Joanne was expecting a baby. Joanne's Catholic father was very angry that she was with a Muslim man. And there was more bad news: Joanne's father was dying. She didn't want to marry Abdulfattah and upset her father at this difficult time.

In those days, life was extremely hard for unmarried women with children, so Joanne decided to offer the baby for adoption. She was very clear about one thing: she wanted her baby to go to parents who had studied at university.

Her baby boy was born in San Francisco on February the 24th, 1955. He was adopted by Paul and Clara Jobs, a kind, quiet couple who had hoped for children for ten years. They called the baby Steven.

When Joanne found out that Paul and Clara had both left school at an early age, she refused to sign the adoption papers. But the baby seemed happy with his new parents, and after a few weeks Joanne changed her mind. However, the Jobs had to promise that they would send Steve to university.

Paul and Clara enjoyed being parents. Two years after Steve arrived in their lives, they adopted another child, a baby girl called Patty.

As a young child, Steve was usually awake at four in the morning, and his interest in everything around him often got him into trouble. But Paul Jobs was a calm, patient father. He was also skilled at making things. If furniture was needed for the house, Paul made it in the garage. He invited his son to help. He also gave him a part of the garage where he could make his own things.

Paul Jobs loved to buy and mend old cars as a hobby. Then he sold them for more money than he had spent on them. Steve watched his father work on the cars, but he didn't really want to get his own hands dirty. The cars sometimes needed work on their electronics, however, and this interested Steve much more. He also loved the trips to the junkyard to buy old car parts. His father seemed to know more than the people that worked there, so he always bought the parts for a good price.

The family were now living in Mountain View, a town in the Santa Clara valley. This part of California was famous for all its technology companies. Innovations in electronics and early computing were happening there. In the 1970s people started to call the area Silicon Valley because microchips, an important part of computers, are usually made of silicon.

Many of the Jobs' neighbours were scientists and electronics experts. One of them, Larry Lang, worked at the technology company Hewlett-Packard. He saw that Steve was an intelligent young boy and he taught him how to make radios and other electronic toys.

Home life was very happy for Steve, but at school he was often bored. If he wasn't interested in something, he refused to do any work on it. He played lots of tricks on the children and teachers, and several times he was sent home early from school.

When Steve was about ten, his school realised that he was very clever. They decided that he should learn with older kids. But this meant a new school in a more dangerous part of town. There were lots of fights at the new school, and Steve had problems with the other children. After a year, he refused to go back. His parents decided to move the family five kilometres down the valley to a town called Cupertino. The schools were better there, and Steve was happier. Most of his friends were older than him and shared his love for maths, science and electronics.

Steve in his high school electronics class.

Steve often went back to Mountain View to visit Mr Lang. At Lang's suggestion, Steve joined the Hewlett-Packard Explorers Club. Different Hewlett-Packard scientists came to the club to talk, and everyone had to build a machine. For Steve's machine, he needed some expensive Hewlett-Packard parts. One night,

twelve-year-old Steve phoned Bill Packard, the CEO*
of this huge company, at his home and explained what
he wanted. Twenty minutes later, Packard had not only
promised to give Steve the parts for free, but also offered
him a job for the summer holidays.

The work that summer wasn't very exciting, but Steve
loved spending time at Hewlett-Packard. He also worked
in an electronics shop called Haltek. Haltek was a junkyard
for old and unwanted electronics. Jobs learnt a lot there.
He started buying things cheaply at electronics markets in
other towns and selling them for more money to his boss at
Haltek. His life as an entrepreneur had begun.

Around this time, Steve Jobs first met Steve Wozniak
– usually known as Woz to his friends. Woz had been
at Steve's school a few years before, and was famous
for knowing more about electronics than the electronics
teacher. In his free time, Woz was building his own
computer with the help of his younger neighbour Bill
Fernandez, a school friend of Steve Jobs. When Steve came
to see the computer, he and Woz started talking. They both
loved electronics and they both loved the music of Bob
Dylan. Woz was five years older than Steve, but they were
soon close friends.

Steve learned electronics at high school, but he wasn't
the star of the class like Woz had been. He began to realise
that electronics was not the only exciting thing in life. He
discovered a love for the great thinkers and writers of the
past, including Shakespeare and Plato. His interest in both
science and the arts was unusual. Unlike most people in
technology, Steve understood those who had no interest
at all in electronics. Later, Apple products were the first
choice for creative people like designers and musicians.

* The CEO (Chief Executive Officer) is the head of the company.

At high school Steve also started a relationship with a girl called Chris-Ann Brennan. She was making her own animated film and wasn't interested in anything that the school could teach her. She and Steve agreed on many things and spent a lot of time together.

Steve didn't often go to school, but when he was there he still liked to play tricks on people! With expert electronics help from his new friend Woz, the tricks worked extremely well, and Steve was often in trouble with the teachers.

Then Woz suggested another type of trick. He had read about a machine called a 'blue box'. By making the right noises down the phone lines, a blue box could trick the phone company so you could make free phone calls to anywhere in the world. Steve and Woz decided to make their own blue box. At first, they made changes to the machine that Steve had built when he went to the Explorer Club, but it didn't work very well. Instead, Woz decided to make a digital blue box. When it was finished, he drove to Steve's house to give it a try. It worked!

The blue box

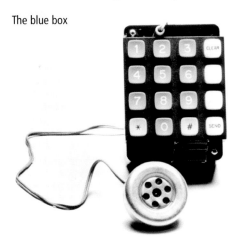

At first they used it to play tricks on people. Woz even phoned the Pope* in Rome, pretending to be an important American politician. But he was told that it was 5.30 a.m. in Italy and the Pope was sleeping. Then Steve suggested a new idea – an idea that later changed their lives. They could make lots of these blue boxes and sell them.

Woz had created the electronics for the blue box, but Steve now wanted a case and other parts for it so that people could use it easily. Steve knew how to get these parts for about $40 a box. He decided to sell the finished box for $150.

Woz was studying at Berkeley University so Steve showed some Berkeley students how to use the blue box. Soon everyone wanted one. Steve and Woz sold about a hundred, and started asking $300 for a box if the buyers looked rich. But then the telephone company found out about their little business and worse followed. Steve showed one of the boxes to a man in a pizza restaurant, and the man asked to buy one. Outside the restaurant, however, he pointed a gun at Steve and stole the box from him. It seemed like a sign. Steve and Woz decided to stop selling the boxes before they got into any serious trouble.

Their adventure with the blue boxes didn't last very long, but it was an important first step into the world of business. They learned how to work together. Woz could create amazing things with electronics. Steve could make Woz's creations easy for people to use, and find people to buy them. They made a great team.

* The Pope is the head of the Catholic Church.

Chapter 2
The birth of Apple

Paul and Clara Jobs had promised Steve's birth mother that they would send him to university, and in 1972 that time had come. There were some great choices locally, like Stanford and Berkeley. Steve told his parents, however, that only one university was right for him: Reed College in Oregon. It was an arts university, and was one of the most expensive places to study in the country. His parents didn't have a lot of money, but they finally agreed to send him there.

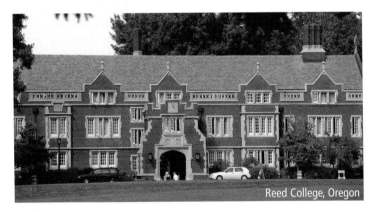
Reed College, Oregon

At Reed, Steve learned little in class. Instead, he and his new friend Daniel Kottke became interested in Zen Buddhism. Steve stopped wearing shoes and stopped eating meat. Sometimes, he ate nothing at all for a week, and at other times lived on only fruit and green vegetables. He continued to be a vegetarian for the rest of his life.

After a term, Steve decided to stop his studies. He didn't think they were worth the money that his parents were paying. He didn't want to leave Reed, however. He stayed there with Daniel and his other friends and went to a few classes that interested him. He went to dance classes to meet girls and he also went to a class where he was taught different styles of handwriting. Later, this class was the reason Steve introduced a choice of writing styles on Apple computers. Computers hadn't offered a choice before.

In 1974, Steve moved back to his parents' house and started looking for a job. Atari was a young company in Silicon Valley that, two years before, had produced the world's first successful computer game – a very simple, black and white form of computer tennis called Pong. One day Al Alcorn, the boss of Atari, was told, 'There's a guy here who won't leave until we employ him.' Alcorn agreed to meet him: an eighteen-year-old Steve Jobs with old clothes, no shoes and a bad smell. But he liked Steve's excitement about technology and offered him a job.

Steve usually worked at night in the Atari office. His manager didn't want him to be there during the day because he smelled so bad. Steve made some useful changes to the games that he worked on, but he was soon looking for a new adventure.

He was very interested in the religions of the East, so he decided to go to India with his friend, Daniel Kottke. They stayed in small Indian villages and met Hindu teachers. But Steve found that he learnt more from ordinary Indian villagers than from the teachers. In the USA, people depended on facts to help them understand things. In these villages, people depended on their feelings instead. Steve learnt to use both ways of thinking.

After seven months in India, Steve returned home, but he continued to find out about religion. He found a Zen teacher, Kobun Chino Otogawa, who helped him to choose a path for his life.

Steve attended a few science classes at Stanford University. He also spent a lot of time working at an apple farm in Oregon that was owned by one of his friends from Reed. But this work was unpaid. Soon he returned to his night job at Atari.

Woz was now working at Hewlett-Packard and had an apartment near the Atari office. While Steve was working, Woz used to come and play the new games in the office. Then, if Steve had a problem, Woz was there to help. Atari was pleased with Steve's work and gave him his own game to design. His boss said that he could earn extra money if he could design it with less than fifty microchips.

Steve knew that he would need Woz's help for this. He offered him half the money, and they worked right through the night for four nights. Finally the game was finished – with only forty-five microchips. Many years later, Woz was upset to find out that Steve kept much more than half the money for the game.

Woz then asked Steve to look at his latest creation: a small computer, keyboard and screen that could all sit together on a desk – a PC or personal computer. No one had made anything like it before, and Steve understood that it could be an important innovation. He suggested that they turned this personal computer into a business. Woz didn't want to leave his job at Hewlett-Packard, and he wasn't terribly interested in making money. But he loved the idea of having a business with his best friend.

The new company needed a name. Steve suggested 'Apple' after a visit to his friend's apple farm. He liked it because it didn't sound technological, and because Apple came before Atari in the phone book! They decided to use that name if they couldn't think of anything better by the end of the day. They couldn't, so on April the 1st, 1976, Apple Computers was born.

When Steve and Woz presented their ideas for a personal computer to the local computer club, one man was very interested. His name was Paul Terrell and he owned a computer shop. Steve went to see him the next day and came back with an order for fifty computers. This was fantastic news, but there was a problem. The parts cost about $15,000. Steve and Woz had only $1300.

They asked the bank for some money, but the bank didn't want to lend to these two young people. Steve offered his old workplace, Haltek, a share in Apple Computers in return for the parts. Haltek said no. Finally, a different shop agreed to give Steve and Woz the parts. They had thirty days before they had to pay for them.

Steve and Woz used the Jobs' house and garage as a

factory. Woz didn't have much time because he was still working at Hewlett-Packard. But with some help from Daniel Kottke, his girlfriend Elizabeth, and Steve's sister Patty, the computers were built before the end of the thirty days. They had managed the impossible. The new product – Apple I – went on sale.

APPLE PRODUCTS:
Apple I (1976)

The Apple I was sold with all the necessary microchips, which was unusual for computers in those days. But customers had to add their own case, keyboard and screen!

Only two hundred of these were ever made.

The Apple I computer. The box was made by a customer.

Now Steve and Woz had enough money to buy parts for a hundred more Apple I computers. The business was going well. But Steve wanted to sell thousands of computers, not a hundred. He decided to take the Apple I to the Personal Computer Fair on the east coast of the USA. All the important people in the computer industry planned to be there. Some of them might take an interest in the Apple I.

At the fair, Apple was given a small table at the back of the hall. The Apple I was there in a wooden case, but few people came to see it. The trip was not a success. Steve walked around the hall sadly. He felt sure that they had the best computer at the fair. But he realised that it didn't look very interesting. He decided that they needed to sell a computer with its own screen and keyboard, and in an attractive case. They also needed a bigger space at the front of the hall.

Woz was already working on a better computer, the Apple II. To make Woz's next computer a success, they were going to need a lot more money.

Chapter 3
A computer in colour

'About half of the difference between successful entrepreneurs and unsuccessful ones is determination.'
Steve Jobs

Woz had some exciting ideas for the electronics of the Apple II. He had even found a way to show information on the computer screen in colour. It was the first time that anyone had managed to do this.

Steve worked on ideas for the computer's case. He also wanted to find a better way to keep the computer cool. Inside most computers there were noisy machines to do this. He and Woz knew almost nothing about this side of computer design, so they employed someone who did. His name was Rod Holt, and his clever new ideas made computers much quieter. Today they are almost silent.

Steve and Woz needed someone to put some serious money into the business. Producing the Apple II was going to cost much more than the Apple I. Steve asked a lot of people for money, but he wore old clothes and no shoes to meetings. Everyone said no.

Then Steve and Woz met Mike Markkula. Mike was only thirty-three, but he had worked at other computer companies and made a lot of money. He thought the Apple II had a big future. He decided to join Apple and put $250,000 into the company.

Many of Steve's ideas about business were learnt from Mike. They both believed that it was better to make a few products really well than to make lots of products. They also believed that the presentation of a product was almost as important as the product itself.

Woz finally agreed to leave his job at Hewlett-Packard. A few programmers started working for Apple too – some of them high school students. Everyone had a lot to do before the presentation of the Apple II at the West Coast Computer Fair in San Francisco.

Steve had learnt from his mistake at the last fair. This time he paid for an area at the front of the hall, and also spent a lot of money to make sure it looked good. When the fair opened in April 1977, the visitors' first sight was of three Apple IIs, each in an attractive and simple plastic case. Behind the computers there was a big picture of an apple in bright colours. Steve and Woz had even agreed to wear suits! Apple looked like the most exciting company at the fair. Everyone wanted to try its amazing new computers with their colour screens.

Apple got three hundred orders at the fair. It was an even better result than they had hoped for. Soon software companies produced some great office software for it and it quickly became the most popular computer in the world. It was used not only in offices, but also in some US schools and homes. For many people, it was the first computer that they ever saw. Almost six million Apple II computers were sold during the sixteen years that it was produced.

APPLE PRODUCTS:
Apple II (1977)

The Apple II was the first computer that could show information on a screen in colour.

The plastic case covered both the keyboard and the electronics.

By the end of 1977, Apple was a very successful business. It moved out of the Jobs' garage and into an office of its own. But Steve was a difficult person to work with. He wanted everything to be perfect. He shouted at the programmers and used a lot of bad language. He told people that their work was terrible, when sometimes he just didn't understand it. He still believed that, because he ate only fruit, he only had to wash once a week. He smelled really bad.

Mike Markkula and Woz decided to employ a new CEO who could manage Steve. They chose Mike Scott. He was a friend of Mike Markkula's, and he was as determined as Steve was. He said no to many of Steve's expensive and unnecessary ideas for making a perfect product. For example, the case of the Apple II was a very pale brown. The plastics factory already offered two thousand pale brown colours, but Steve wanted something new. Mike Scott said that the cost of this was too high. Steve hated him. They shouted and screamed at each other, and sometimes Steve even cried. The Apple office was never a quiet place.

Home life was not very quiet for Steve either. He had moved out of his parents' home and was living with Daniel Kottke and Chris-Ann Brennan, his girlfriend from high school. Since their school days, Steve and Chris-Ann had stayed friends. Now, living in the same house, their relationship started again. Soon Chris-Ann was expecting Steve's baby. They were both twenty-three – the same age that Steve's parents had been when Steve arrived.

Steve wasn't ready to be a dad. He decided not to believe Chris-Ann. Perhaps he really thought that someone else might be the father, or perhaps he was just lying to himself and his friends. Chris-Ann was very angry with him. She moved to the apple farm in Oregon where she and Steve had spent a lot of time together, and there she had a baby girl. Steve went to meet the baby and gave her a name, Lisa. But then he did nothing to help. He was a rich man now. Chris-Ann was very poor, but Steve didn't give any of his money to her and the baby.

A few years later, Steve did a test to check if he was really Lisa's father. It was quite clear that he was. He then gave Chris-Ann a home and paid for a good school for Lisa, but he spent very little time with her. Later in his life, he felt really bad about this.

At the time, Apple was the only 'child' that Steve was interested in. The Apple II was still selling well, but this couldn't last forever. And everyone knew that Woz, not Steve, had been the main creator of the Apple II. Steve wanted to create a new computer himself – a better computer than any that had come before it. He chose a team of fantastic people and started work on a new computer. Strangely, he called it 'the Lisa'.

Without Woz's genius, however, things didn't go well at first. So Steve decided that he needed some new ideas. He found them at a big technology company called Xerox. Xerox wanted to buy shares in Apple. Jobs agreed to this, but asked in return to meet the company's computer scientists. When he saw the computers that these scientists had created, he was really excited. To give instructions to computers at that time, you had to use a difficult computer language. But one of the scientists' ideas was something called a 'mouse'. With the mouse, you could choose pictures or words on the screen, and these gave the computer its instructions. It was so easy that a child could do it. Surprisingly, Xerox had no plans to sell computers with these innovations. Steve felt sure that with ideas like these and design from Apple, the Lisa would be the perfect computer for people's homes.

Steve was determined to create something great, but he was rude and unkind to his team at Apple. The shouting and the disagreements never stopped. Finally, Mike Markkula and Mike Scott decided that Steve must stop work on the Lisa. Steve was very upset.

He had other things to think about, however. Apple was planning to become a 'public company'. This meant selling millions of small shares in the company to the public. It was a useful way to get more money so that the company could grow. The shares went on sale in December 1980 and they were very popular. The price went up and up. When Mike Markkula had joined Apple in early 1977, the company was worth $5,309. At the end of 1980, it was worth $1.79 billion. Some people at Apple kept shares for themselves and three hundred people in the company suddenly became millionaires. Steve, at the age of twenty-five, had $256 million.

Steve gave some of his money to his parents, but he didn't share much of it. He didn't spend very much either. He bought a nice car, a very expensive music player and a huge house. But he couldn't find the perfect furniture for the house, so the house stayed almost empty.

Woz (left) and Steve in Steve's house

The newspapers loved the young Steve Jobs, the face of the USA's most successful company since the 1950s. He appeared on the cover of several magazines and became Silicon Valley's most famous name.

Chapter 4
The first Mac

'My job is not to be easy on people. My job is to take great people and to push them and make them even better.'
Steve Jobs

Other people were now managing the Lisa, so Steve needed something else to work on. He chose the Macintosh. It was a computer that Apple hoped to sell for under $1000. This was cheap enough for smaller businesses and college students.

Mike Scott left Apple in 1981, and Mike Markkula became CEO. Markkula didn't like disagreements, so he usually let the managers at Apple do what they wanted. This was great news for Steve. He was now able to manage the work on the Macintosh exactly as he wished.

He chose the best people at Apple to work with him and employed some of the scientists from Xerox too. They were told to have the Macintosh ready for sale in one year. This was impossible – everyone knew it except Steve. But Steve had achieved impossible things in the past, like the game that he and Woz had created for Atari in just four days. He believed that the impossible was possible. Some people that worked with him started to believe it too.

But life was difficult for everyone in Steve's team. He was often angry and often rude. If someone had a new idea, Steve usually said that it was stupid. But a couple of days later, he might suggest the same idea, believing that he had thought of it himself. Some people were brave enough to disagree with him, though, and others went quietly ahead with a plan even if Steve had told them not to. Steve liked these people better than the people who always said yes.

Steve didn't want the Macintosh to be just a computer that could do its job and make money for the company. It should also be a work of art. Everything was designed again and again: the case, the pictures and shapes on the screen, even the box that the computer was sold in. The computer had to start up quickly. It had to have a wide choice of writing styles. It had to be really easy to use. In fact, it had to be perfect.

Steve's team worked very hard on the Macintosh and more and more time was spent on it. When the Lisa went on sale in 1983, the Macintosh was still at least a year from completion. Steve talked to reporters about the Lisa, but he also talked about Apple's future product, the Macintosh. He told them it was a cheaper computer with amazing programs that couldn't run on the Lisa. His words killed all hope of good sales for the Lisa. This was terrible news for Apple.

Soon after this, Mike Markkula decided to leave his position as CEO of Apple. Steve wanted the job one day, but he wasn't ready yet. Apple needed someone older, an expert in selling products. They chose John Sculley.

Sculley was the CEO of the drinks company PepsiCo, and he was happy where he was. At first he wasn't sure that he wanted to join Apple. He was interested in Steve, however, and in Steve's strong belief in changing the way people used computers. Steve asked him, 'Do you want to spend the rest of your life selling sugared water? Or do you want a chance to change the world?' For Sculley, the answer was clear.

In 1983, Sculley moved to California as Apple's CEO. For the first few months, he and Steve were good friends and worked closely together. But then the problems started.

Steve with John Sculley in 1984

The Macintosh was planned at first as a $1000
computer, but with all Steve's changes the price had risen
to $1995. Now Sculley said that it had to sell for $2495
if Steve wanted any money for adverts. This was too
expensive for ordinary people and Steve was very angry.
But he couldn't change Sculley's mind.

Apple needed the Macintosh to be a big success. Sales
of the Apple II were slowing, and the Lisa had failed
badly. The big technology company IBM's personal
computer was now selling much faster than Apple's,
and its Microsoft operating system was also used on
other companies' computers. Apple's operating systems,
however, were only allowed on Apple computers. Apple
was in danger of becoming a forgotten part of computer
history.

In 1984, Steve employed the famous Hollywood
director Ridley Scott to make an advert for the Macintosh.
In the advert, a political leader on a huge screen tells a
crowd of workers in grey clothes that they all have the
same wishes and the same thoughts. Then a girl runs into

the room, wearing a t-shirt with a picture of a Macintosh on it. She throws something at the screen and breaks the glass. The message is clear: the Macintosh will free creative people from the narrow choice of an IBM-style computer.

The advert was one minute long. Apple paid to show it on TV once only, because many people at the company didn't like it. But once was enough. The public loved it. It was like no advert that they had seen before. It was shown again and again on the evening news around the country.

Two days after the TV advert was shown, there was a big meeting for shareholders and reporters. Steve was always good at public speaking. He could keep the attention of a crowd for hours with his interesting stories and funny jokes. Now he told everyone about the Macintosh, and showed them the great things that it could do. Then the Macintosh itself started speaking. It told a joke about IBM before introducing 'the man who has been like a father to me: Steve Jobs.' The crowd went wild. It was the cleverest computer that they had ever seen. Soon computer shops were full of people wanting to buy the new computer. The first three months' sales of the Macintosh, or Macs, were fantastic.

Not all the people who bought the Mac were happy, however. If you bought an IBM PC, you had a wide choice of software, but you could use almost none of it on a Mac. Customers were also unhappy that the screen was small and not in colour. The Mac didn't have enough power, so it was very slow. Too often, it stopped working completely.

By spring 1985, Apple were only selling a tenth of the Macs that they had hoped to sell. Woz had left to start a new company, and many of the best people from the

Macintosh team were leaving too. Apple's directors felt that their problems were the fault of Steve Jobs. He was a bad manager of people. He had stopped the Lisa from being successful. Now even the Macintosh was failing.

APPLE PRODUCTS:
The Macintosh (1984)

The screen was small and in black and white, but you could use a lot of different writing styles.

The case and keyboard didn't need much space on a desk.

The Macintosh was one of the first computers to have a mouse.

Sculley decided to take Steve off the Macintosh team. Instead, he told him to work on ideas for new products. Steve was angry that people didn't like his management style. He secretly made a plan with some friends to throw Sculley out of Apple and become CEO himself. But Sculley found out. He told the Apple directors that he couldn't work with Steve anymore. Either he or Steve had to go. The directors chose to keep Sculley and Steve lost his job as a director of the company that he had started.

Chapter 5
Starting again

*'I didn't see it then, but losing my job at Apple was
the best thing that ever happened to me.'*
Steve Jobs

Steve was very upset. For days, he stayed at home and
spoke to no one except his girlfriend, Tina. Then he started
to think seriously about his future. He was only thirty.
What should he do with the rest of his life?

At first he thought about becoming a politician. But
he found technology more interesting than politics as a
way to change the world. He was offered several jobs as
a university teacher, but he said no to them all. But one
conversation with a university scientist was very useful.
'Our work is moving too slowly,' the scientist said. 'The
problems would disappear if we had personal computers
that were more powerful.'

This was the idea that Steve was looking for. He
decided to start a new company that made computers
powerful enough for use in universities.

A few of his old team at Apple wanted to leave their
jobs and work with Steve. He sold his shares in Apple,
and his new company, NeXT, was born.

There was other exciting news in his life. After years
of searching, he found and met his birth mother, Joanne
Schieble, in Los Angeles. The two stayed in touch, and in
later years, when she was old, Steve paid for her care.

Joanne told him that she and his father, Abdulfattah
Jandali, had finally married and had another child,
Mona. Five years later, Abdulfattah had left his family,
and Joanne had married again. Mona now called herself

Mona Simpson, and was a writer in New York. When Steve and his new sister met, they found that they were very similar. They went for a long walk – something that they both enjoyed – and talked for hours. Mona liked Steve immediately. Steve had never been very close to his adopted sister, Patty, but Steve and Mona were close for the rest of Steve's life.

Mona Simpson

Mona also found their father. Steve wasn't interested in meeting him. He didn't like the fact that this man had left Mona when she was only five. But Mona wanted to see him again. He was the manager of a small restaurant north of San Francisco, and he told her about a bigger restaurant that he had managed in the past in Silicon Valley. 'All the successful technology people used to come there,' he told his daughter. 'Even Steve Jobs. He was a sweet guy.' It was hard for Mona, but she said nothing. She had to keep her brother's secret. Steve never went to visit Abdulfattah.

As well as NeXT, Steve started another company. George Lucas, the director of the Star Wars films, had sold Steve the computer animation side of his business. Steve gave this business the name Pixar and planned to sell the hugely powerful and expensive computers that it had designed for use in animation.

Steve's main job, however, was at NeXT, and unfortunately he hadn't learnt many lessons from his years at Apple. He was still rude and unkind to many of his workers, and to people in other companies. Steve spent lots of money on a beautiful new design for the NeXT offices, and on an attractive, modern factory. But there were huge problems with the computer that the factory produced.

Steve at NeXT product presentation, 1988

As always with Steve, the design of the computer had to be perfect. Of course, the perfect computer takes a very long time to create. When Steve finally showed it to reporters in 1988, it was two years late, and it wasn't even finished. People had to wait another six months for a computer that they could use. And worse, it cost $6500. Few universities could pay more than $3000 for a personal computer, so it sold very badly.

However, the NeXT computer had one important fan. Computer scientist Tim Berners-Lee used it to create something that truly changed the world: the World Wide Web. Because the machine was so powerful, this huge job only took him a couple of months.

The Pixar computers were selling as badly as the NeXT ones, but the company had some success in another area. It had employed an animator, John Lasseter, to show everyone the amazing animation that the Pixar computers and software could produce. In 1989, Lasseter's short film, *Tin Toy*, won an Oscar*.

* Oscars are given by the US film industry to the best films and actors of the year.

CHAPTER 6
A family man

'Things don't have to change the world to be important.'
Steve Jobs

As a young man, Steve had plenty of beautiful and intelligent girlfriends, including Chris-Ann and the famous singer Joan Baez. Another girlfriend, Tina Redse, had helped him through the difficult days when he was thrown out of Apple, but she and Steve sometimes had terrible fights. Five years after the start of their relationship, Steve asked her to marry him, but she decided that it couldn't work.

Steve and Laurene in their Palo Alto home

Everything changed for Steve when he met Laurene Powell in 1989. He was giving a talk at Stanford University, and she was a business student there. After a short conversation, he arranged to take her to dinner that Saturday. As he drove away from Stanford, he changed his mind. He couldn't wait until Saturday. Although he had a work dinner that night, he didn't go. Instead, he and Laurene went to a vegetarian restaurant together.

They stayed together. The early days of their relationship were not smooth, and sometimes Steve thought about going back to Tina. He asked Laurene to marry him, and then he changed his mind. Finally, the two were married in 1991 by Steve's Zen teacher, Kobun Chino. It was a quiet wedding with only fifty guests.

Steve and Laurene chose to live in a large but fairly normal home in a nice part of Palo Alto in Silicon Valley. It was near the NeXT offices, and it was a safe and friendly place for children. This was important because Laurene was expecting a baby.

Their son, Reed, was born in 1991. A year later, Steve's fourteen-year-old daughter, Lisa, joined the family after some problems with her mother. As a young child, Lisa had almost never seen her dad. But Steve had started to take an interest in Lisa as she got older. She was an intelligent girl, but as determined as her father. Sometimes they were close, but at other times they had big fights. When she left home and became a writer, she and Steve sometimes didn't speak for years.

Steve with Lisa in 1989

Steve's next daughter, Erin, was born in 1995, and her sister, Eve, followed three years later. Laurene managed a vegetarian food business when she first married, but soon stopped work so that she could spend time with the kids. Although work often kept Steve away from home, he was careful to make time for them too. If they rang him when he was in a meeting, he was always ready to speak to them. The family went on lots of nice holidays in Hawaii, and enjoyed time on the expensive boats of Steve's business friends. Later, when he had many billions of dollars, Steve had a private plane, but his way of life was surprisingly simple.

Steve loved his work and his family, but he had many other interests. He enjoyed cycling, skiing, sailing and walking in the California hills. He loved travelling, too. Paris and Kyoto were two of his favourite cities.

* * *

Around the time of Steve and Laurene's wedding, there was exciting news from Pixar. The company was planning a film with Disney. Pixar would make the film, with John Lasseter as director, and Disney would pay for it. The film, *Toy Story*, was about toys who wanted their owner to play with them.

The people at Disney loved the idea of the film, but they weren't happy with the story. Every time they saw Lasseter's work, they asked for changes. After Lasseter made all these changes, the Disney people were still unhappy. They decided not to go ahead with the film.

Steve, however, believed that Lasseter could make *Toy Story* fantastic. He decided to put some more of his own money into the film. Interestingly, he didn't suggest changes as he always did with computers. He knew that he wasn't an expert in the film industry. Three months later, he and Lasseter returned to Disney with some new ideas for the film, and this time the Disney bosses were happy.

Toy Story arrived in cinemas in time for the winter holidays of 1995. It was a huge success. One week later, Pixar shares went on sale, and they were amazingly popular. Suddenly, Steve's share of Pixar was worth $1.2 billion – twenty times more than he had ever put into the company.

But Pixar was starting to achieve something much more important to Steve than money. It was becoming a company that every family in the world had heard of. By the time of Steve's death, Pixar had made twelve very successful films and won twenty-six Oscars.

Chapter 7
'Think different!'

'I'm as proud of what we don't do as I am of what we do.'
Steve Jobs

The 1984 Macintosh had not sold well, but its operating system – with windows and pictures – was hugely popular because it was so easy to use. Since Steve had left Apple, there had been new Macs with the same operating system, and these had been more successful. But there had also been a lot of less successful products, including digital cameras and CD players. By 1996, Microsoft's operating system, Windows, was almost as good as the Mac's. Windows computers were usually cheaper than Apple machines, and had a much bigger choice of software. Apple was still popular with creative people like designers and artists, but every year it had a smaller share of the general computer market.

John Sculley had left Apple in 1993, and Gil Amelio was now the CEO. He decided that Apple computers needed a new operating system. When his software people failed to produce anything good enough, he looked at other companies with an operating system that Apple could buy. One of them was NeXT.

NeXT was not enjoying the same success as Pixar. In 1993, Steve had had to close the side of the business that made computers. Now it just produced software. Its NeXTSTEP operating system seemed to be a good choice for Apple. But would Steve agree to sell it to his old company?

Amelio was surprised by his answer. He wanted to sell not just the operating system but the whole company. 'We have good software and a great team,' he said. 'You can have us all.' In 1997, Apple bought NeXT for $400 million, and Steve was employed to 'give advice' to Apple.

Steve made sure that his best people from NeXT were given good jobs at Apple. But his own job there was only part-time. He wasn't a director, so he wasn't invited to the company's most important meetings. For Steve, this was very difficult. Apple was losing money fast, and a lot of its best people were leaving. Changes were needed urgently, but Amelio didn't seem to have a clear plan.

Six months after Apple bought NeXT, Amelio was thrown out. Steve was asked to become a director, and soon he was making big changes. If any of the directors disagreed with him, they were also thrown out of the company. A month after Amelio left, Apple had an almost completely new group of directors – most of them friends of Steve's. A month after that, Steve became CEO.

Apple fans were very happy. For the first time in many years, the company had a strong leader with innovative ideas.

Steve wanted to make customers and workers at Apple believe in the company again. He asked for help from the people who had created the 1984 Macintosh advert. They made a new advert called 'Think Different'.

It showed no Apple products. Instead, there was black and white film of famous people – Picasso, Einstein, Gandhi, Bob Dylan and many more. The words of the advert talked about the people that everyone called 'crazy' – the people with new ideas that change the world. 'While some may see them as the crazy ones,' said the advert, 'we see genius.' The advert was a huge success. It was a sign to the computer industry, and to the world, that Apple's creative genius was back.

It wasn't an easy time at Apple, however. In 1997 – Steve's first year back at the company – about 3000 workers lost their jobs. People were scared to get into a lift with Steve. While the lift went up or down a few floors, he asked about their work. If he didn't like their answers, he told them to leave the company.

More than half of Apple's products came to a sudden end. Steve wanted computers to become Apple's main business again, with only a few really good computers to choose from.

Steve decided that all work at Apple should be secret. The company made careful plans for giving information to reporters at the right time. No one else was allowed to talk about new products. If they did, they had to leave Apple immediately. Later, these rules helped to increase the excitement about new products from Apple. On the Internet, people spent a lot of time guessing the type of product that was coming next.

Very quickly Steve's actions started to bring results for the company. In the year before he became CEO, Apple lost more than a billion dollars. In the year after his return, it made money.

Steve gave most of his attention to Apple's new home computer. He wanted a machine that ordinary people could use easily. Even a young child should be able to get it out of the box and then use the Internet.

As always, the appearance of the computer was very important. Steve looked at lots of people's ideas for the case, but he found them boring. He wanted his designers to 'think different'. A designer from England, Jonathan Ive, suggested a bright blue case in an unusual shape, a bit like an egg. Steve loved the idea. Of course, the design had many changes before Steve was completely happy with it. He visited the design room at the end of every work day. He and Jonathan made a good team, and they worked on many more designs together.

Steve often asked for the impossible, as he had done before. But in one important way he was different. He understood that things couldn't always be perfect. When he saw the way that CDs went in and out of the new computer, he was very upset. This wasn't what he had wanted. But he didn't make everyone change the design. The new computer, called the iMac, was ready on time.

Designer Jonathan Ive (left) with the iMac

It went on sale in 1998. It was much cheaper than Apple's other computers, and it sold even faster than the

Apple II. Importantly, almost half of its customers were buying their first computer or had only used a Windows machine before. After many years of problems, Apple had finally produced another successful product.

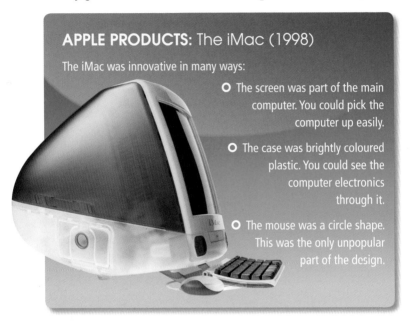

APPLE PRODUCTS: The iMac (1998)

The iMac was innovative in many ways:

O The screen was part of the main computer. You could pick the computer up easily.

O The case was brightly coloured plastic. You could see the computer electronics through it.

O The mouse was a circle shape. This was the only unpopular part of the design.

Chapter 8
'1000 songs in your pocket'

'People don't know what they want until you show it to them.'
Steve Jobs

By 2000, Apple was making a lot of money. In 2001, the company opened its own shops in several American cities. Steve put a lot of thought into the design of these shops, and they brought in huge numbers of new customers. More shops were planned for cities around the world.

Steve Jobs loved music – Bob Dylan, the Beatles and many more – and he knew that people were starting to listen to music as MP3s. He wanted Apple's computers to share in this new MP3 technology. In 2001, the company introduced iTunes, a great piece of software that helped you to organise your digital music into playlists for your MP3 player. But Steve soon realised that he hated all the MP3 players that you could buy at the time. They were difficult to use, and only held about sixteen songs. He decided that Apple should create something better.

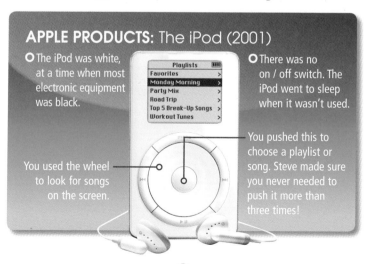

APPLE PRODUCTS: The iPod (2001)

○ The iPod was white, at a time when most electronic equipment was black.

Playlists
Favorites >
Monday Morning >
Party Mix >
Road Trip >
Top 5 Break-Up Songs >
Workout Tunes >

○ There was no on / off switch. The iPod went to sleep when it wasn't used.

You pushed this to choose a playlist or song. Steve made sure you never needed to push it more than three times!

You used the wheel to look for songs on the screen.

He got some help from a small company called PortalPlayer, and there were lots of ideas from people at Apple, including Jonathan Ive and Steve himself. Their product, the iPod, could hold a thousand songs, but fitted easily inside your pocket. 'We knew how cool it was,' remembered Steve, 'because we knew how badly we wanted one ourselves.'

It took the company less than a year to design and produce the iPod. When it first went on sale, however, reporters did not like it. 'No one will buy it,' they said. 'It's much too expensive.' But they were wrong. Soon young people all around the world were buying iPods. Apple's brightly-coloured iPod adverts were everywhere.

The success didn't stop there. The company was now working hard on a new idea – an idea that changed the world of music forever. In 2002, the music industry was in big trouble. Young people could now share MP3s on music websites for free. Sales of CDs were falling fast. If people stopped paying for music, the music companies would go out of business. They were very worried.

The music companies needed an online shop for their music, but unfortunately the big companies didn't want to work together. There were two different websites, each with only half the songs that people were interested in. And there was another problem: you had to pay every month. If you stopped paying, you lost all the songs that you had already bought. The websites were very unpopular, and people continued to use the free MP3-sharing websites.

For Apple, free music was useful because it made the iPod more attractive. But Steve knew that free MP3s were destroying the music industry. He also felt strongly that stealing other people's creative products was wrong. He thought that most people in the world were honest. They would pay for their music if they could. The problem at the moment was that they had too many excuses to be dishonest. He decided that it was time for an iTunes shop.

Steve started talking to the five biggest music companies about his ideas for this shop. The music had to be cheap – 99 cents for a song – so that customers didn't want to steal anymore. They had to be able to buy one song at a time, not all the songs from a CD. And they had to be able to keep those songs forever.

At first, many of the music companies said no. But Steve was very determined. Slowly, the music companies started to change their minds. They loved Apple's simple and attractive software. But before a website could sell music, it often needed agreement from the musicians too. Steve met with lots of famous singers and bands, such as Bob Dylan,

U2 and Mick Jagger, and talked and talked about Apple's fantastic idea. Finally, enough people agreed to sell their music at his shop.

Steve Jobs with U2

In 2003, the iTunes shop opened. It already had 200,000 songs, and that number was growing every day. Apple expected to sell a million songs in the first six months. Instead, it sold a million songs in the first six days. In 2010, on Steve Jobs' fifty-fifth birthday, the iTunes shop sold its ten billionth song. The lucky buyer, grandfather Louie Sulcer, got a phone call from Steve Jobs to say that he'd won a $10,000 iTunes gift card!

Chapter 9
A phone for the 21st century

'Design is not just what it looks like and feels like. It's how it works.'

Steve Jobs

Apple was now a huge success, but there was terrible news for Steve himself: he had cancer. Doctors said he could have an operation which would probably save his life. If he didn't have the operation, however, he would die.

Steve spoke to his family and a few close friends about his cancer. They all told him to have the operation, but he refused. He had done the impossible many times before, and now he wanted to survive cancer his own way. He looked for ideas on the Internet and decided to try these instead.

He ate only fresh fruit and vegetables and took some natural medicines. But the cancer got worse. Finally, in 2004, he had the operation, but it was nine months too late. By now the cancer had travelled to his liver.

He went back to work soon after the operation. Because of his illness, he was in a hurry to achieve great things for his companies. He sold Pixar to Disney for $7.4 billion. John Lasseter and Pixar's other film makers were given important jobs at Disney, and Steve got a lot of Disney shares. In fact he now had more shares than anyone else.

There was a lot to do at Apple too. Many good products were discussed in meetings and then designed, but only a few – the most exciting and innovative – went on sale. iPods became smaller, were made in brighter colours, and could hold more songs. Some could play video as well as music. They were often selling more quickly than Apple could make them. But Steve was worried. He had seen the fall in digital camera sales when mobile phones with cameras arrived. The same might happen to iPod sales if mobile phones started playing music. Apple needed its own mobile phone.

When Steve started looking at the phones in the shops, he realised that he didn't like any of them. The rest of the team at Apple agreed. But could Apple produce the sort of phone that they would really enjoy using?

It wasn't as easy as they had hoped. The phone team looked at some exciting new technologies. But without the right glass for the screen, their ideas couldn't work. They spoke to glass producers around the world, but no one made anything strong enough. Finally they found a US company that had produced the right type of glass in the 1960s. Few people had bought it, however, so production had stopped. Now Steve told the company to start making as much of this glass as it could.

Steve worked closely with the phone team for six months, always pushing them to make the phone simpler and easier to use. He wasn't the world's greatest designer or software writer. But more than anyone else in the technology industry, he knew what would make a product better for the user.

Two or three times a year Apple organised a big meeting for reporters and technology people. In his blue jeans and black top, Steve would stand at the front and talk with huge excitement about Apple's latest innovations. Millions of people watched Steve's talks on the Internet. The talks were fun and people loved the way that Steve imagined the future.

At one of these meetings in 2007, he told everyone about Apple's world-changing iPhone. Then he phoned Starbucks on an iPhone and ordered 4000 coffees for the people in the room. Everyone loved it!

Reporters said that the iPhone was fun and easy to use, and it looked beautiful. Apple fans were very excited, but they couldn't buy one for six months. People started waiting outside Apple Stores several days before the iPhone went on sale. At the time it was the world's most expensive mobile phone, but some shops had sold all their iPhones after only an hour. By 2010, Apple had sold 90 million iPhones and there was a choice of at least 185,000 apps*. Half of the money from the whole mobile phone market was made by the iPhone.

APPLE PRODUCTS: The iPhone (2007)

○ The iPhone had a new touchscreen that could feel two or more fingers at the same time.

○ You could use the Internet. Using two fingers, you could zoom in on a website.

○ The phone had no keyboard. The screen was almost as big as the phone itself.

What do these words mean?
You can use a dictionary.
touchscreen zoom

* An app is a software program.

Chapter 10
Designing the future

'Death is probably the single best invention of life. …
It clears out the old to make space for the new.'
Steve Jobs

Steve wanted to believe that he did not have cancer, but unfortunately it had not disappeared. He was often in pain, and sometimes he didn't want to eat. In 2008, he almost stopped eating completely and lost a lot of weight.

Steve's doctors told him that he needed a new liver, but there was a long waiting list. When he finally had the operation, it was a success, but there was bad news too. The cancer had travelled to other parts of his body.

He was in hospital for more than two months. At one point everyone thought that he was dying. His children flew in from different parts of the country to say goodbye, but he survived. He was determined to enjoy many more years with the family and businesses that he loved so much.

Even when he was ill in hospital, he was the same Steve. If he didn't like the design of the hospital equipment, he refused to use it. He even drew better designs for some of the machines.

He and his daughter Lisa hadn't talked for several years, but she came to see him now. He was very pleased. He also loved visits from people at Apple, including Jonathan Ive and Tim Cook, the CEO while Steve was ill. He could almost forget his cancer when he was discussing future products with his team.

Finally he returned home. A few days later he was back at the Apple offices for a directors' meeting. He was determined to change the world at least one more time.

Apple's next product was the iPad. The iPad was like a big iPhone. You couldn't make phone calls or send text messages, but it was perfect for reading, using the Internet or playing games. 300,000 were sold on the iPad's first day in the shops. That was even more than the iPhone!

APPLE PRODUCTS:
The iPad (2010)

○ The iPad was about the size of a magazine or an open book and very light.
○ The pictures and video were very clear and in beautiful colour.

But could the iPad change the world, as Steve hoped? He knew that many newspapers and magazines were losing money because people were reading news stories for free on the Internet. He talked to magazine and newspaper bosses about selling their products through apps at the iTunes shop. Perhaps this could save the newspaper industry as it had saved the music industry. But few companies were interested. They wanted to know the email addresses of their readers, and iTunes couldn't give them this.

The book industry, however, was more interested. The iTunes shop already had music, TV shows, films, apps, even university lessons, but no books. This soon changed. From 2010, people could also buy electronic books at iTunes.

There was one important thing that you couldn't find on iTunes: the music of the Beatles. Steve had always loved this band. He was extremely happy when an agreement was finally reached and their songs arrived on iTunes at the end of 2010. He organised some special adverts to celebrate.

Steve's cancer was getting worse. His whole body was in pain, and he had to take a lot of time off work. He always tried to stay optimistic, however. He designed a fantastic boat for his family, and hoped that one day they would travel the world in it together. He knew that the boat builders might not finish it in his lifetime, but he wanted the work to continue. If it stopped, he was accepting his own death. He wanted to keep fighting.

In the last months of his life, he gave lots of advice to young entrepreneurs, including Mark Zuckerberg of Facebook and Larry Page of Google. He even met President Obama and talked about the changes that were needed in US schools. He also made plans for a beautiful new Apple office building in Cupertino, and a TV that Apple might produce in the future.

In June 2011, Steve stood in front of a crowd of reporters and technology people to tell them about Apple's next big thing, the iCloud. This, he said, was the future of technology. You could keep all your work, your emails, your address book, your songs, photos and video on a huge 'computer cloud'. You could see everything on the cloud on your computer, iPod, iPhone or iPad – and it was safe even if you lost or broke one of them.

Steve and Laurene after his talk in June 2011

People were excited about the iCloud, but they were worried about Steve. He was very weak. In August, he realised that he could not continue as Apple's CEO. With great sadness, he gave the job to Tim Cook. He was very hopeful about his company's future, however. 'I believe Apple's brightest and most innovative days are ahead of it,' he said.

Unfortunately, that wasn't true of Steve himself. He was losing his long fight with cancer. Over the years he had had sixty-seven different nurses, and he had been terribly rude to many of them. But he finally found three that he liked, and they stayed with him until the end. On October the 5th, 2011, he died peacefully at his home. His boat was still half-built.

Remembering Steve

TV programmes in the USA were stopped to report the sad news of Steve Jobs' death. Around the world, politicians, business people and friends talked about his amazing achievements and his genius for innovation. Thousands of people left flowers at their nearest Apple shop. Millions wrote messages on the Internet – often using the technology that Steve himself had helped to create.

Chinese students remember Steve outside the Apple offices in Cupertino, California

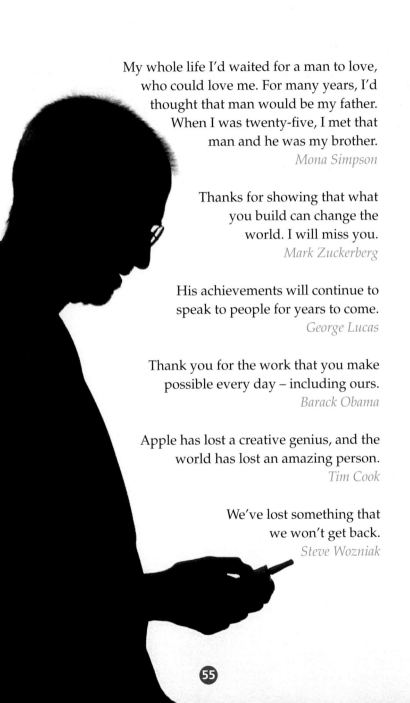

My whole life I'd waited for a man to love,
who could love me. For many years, I'd
thought that man would be my father.
When I was twenty-five, I met that
man and he was my brother.

Mona Simpson

Thanks for showing that what
you build can change the
world. I will miss you.

Mark Zuckerberg

His achievements will continue to
speak to people for years to come.

George Lucas

Thank you for the work that you make
possible every day – including ours.

Barack Obama

Apple has lost a creative genius, and the
world has lost an amazing person.

Tim Cook

We've lost something that
we won't get back.

Steve Wozniak

INVENTIONS
that changed our world

Can you imagine our lives today without these inventions? Life really wouldn't be the same without them!

☐ The wheel
It helps us to travel faster and carry heavy things. It's also used in thousands of machines. Life without wheels? No, thanks!

3500 BC or earlier
▼

☐ The music player
Before 1878, you could only hear music in concerts or read music notes on paper. Thomas Edison's invention allowed many more people to enjoy music.

1878
▼

▲ ▲
1440 1800

▲
1876

☐ The electric battery
Alessandro Volta's battery made electricity, but for a long time there wasn't anything for it to power!

☐ The telephone
Alexander Graham Bell's invention made communication much easier. Soon we were having conversations with people on the other side of the world.

☐ The printing press
Before 1440, books were copied by hand, so they were slow and expensive to produce. Johannes Gutenberg's invention changed all that.

What other important inventions should be on this list?

Film

The first movie was made in England, in black and white and with no sound. It showed some people in a garden. Luckily, films have become a bit more interesting since then!

Television

John Logie Baird's invention changed the way people spent their free time. There are now more than 20,000 TV stations around the world.

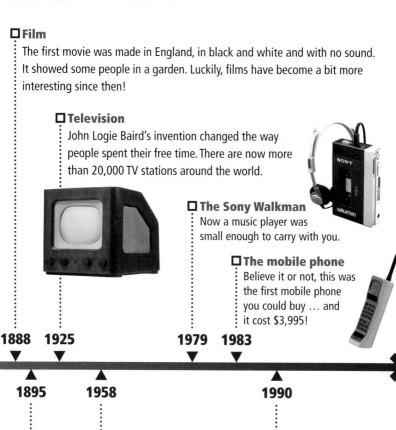

The Sony Walkman

Now a music player was small enough to carry with you.

The mobile phone

Believe it or not, this was the first mobile phone you could buy ... and it cost $3,995!

1888   **1925**   **1979**   **1983**

1895   **1958**   **1990**

The microchip

This tiny American invention is now used in everything from computers to cars, fridges and children's toys.

The World Wide Web

Tim Berners-Lee's invention allowed us to use the Internet easily. Thank you, Tim!

Radio

Guglielmo Marconi was one of many people who helped to invent radio. For half of the twentieth century, it was the main entertainment at home.

What do these words mean? You can use a dictionary.

invent / invention   battery   communication   entertainment   tiny

ENTREPRENEURS
OF THE DIGITAL AGE

Steve Jobs built one of the world's greatest companies. Here are some other entrepreneurs whose business achievements have changed the world.

BILL GATES
Founder of Microsoft

When Bill Gates was young, very few pupils used computers in schools. But Bill's school was different. He was allowed to miss maths classes to write computer programs. His first program was a simple game of Tic Tac Toe*.

In 1975, he and his schoolfriend, Paul Allen, started a software business. Now Microsoft is the biggest software company in the world.

For many years, Bill Gates was the world's richest person. He has given billions of dollars to his charity, the Bill and Melinda Gates Foundation.

* In the game Tic Tac Toe, you have to get three 0s or three Xs in a line.

MARK ZUCKERBERG
Founder of Facebook

Mark Zuckerberg learnt computer programming as a child. When he was twelve, he wrote a program that allowed instant messaging between the computers at his home and his dad's office.

A few years later, Microsoft offered Mark a job, but he went to Harvard University instead. There, in 2004, he started Facebook: a website where Harvard students had their own page with a photo and some information about themselves. After only twenty-four hours, the website had more than 1200 users. Eight years later, that number was 800 million! At the age of twenty-three, Mark was the world's youngest billionaire.

JIMMY WALES
Founder of Wikipedia

At school, Jimmy Wales loved reading encyclopedias. His first job was in finance, but he enjoyed doing computer programming after work. In 2001, Jimmy started an online encyclopedia which later became Wikipedia. The Wikipedia writers weren't paid for their work. Like Jimmy, they wanted to create 'a free encyclopedia for every single person in the world'.

Since it started, Wikipedia has grown and grown. It now has about 100,000 writers, and there are more than 20 million pages in 283 different languages.

> What other entrepreneurs do you know about? What have they achieved?

> **What do these words mean? You can use a dictionary.**
> founder   charity   instant messaging   billionaire   encyclopedia   finance

How to be an

Many people dream of being a successful entrepreneur. But how do you start?

① HAVE A GREAT IDEA

What will your business do? Will it offer help to other people? Or will it produce something: a website, fashion or food? Will it sell the product online, or at a shop or market?

② DO YOUR RESEARCH

You think you've got a fantastic idea, but is anyone else doing the same thing? Before you spend a lot of money on your business, talk to the type of people who you want as your customers. Find out what *they* want.

③ LEARN SMALL BEFORE YOU GO BIG

Being an entrepreneur can be risky. Some people make a lot of money, but others lose a lot. Everyone makes mistakes, so make the risks as small as possible at the start. Steve and Woz produced the Blue Box and the Apple I quite cheaply, and learnt a lot while they were doing this. Then they were confident to spend more on the Apple II.

entrepreneur

④ FIND SOME MONEY

You can't build a big business without money. But that doesn't mean that you have to be rich. If your business idea is good enough, you can find investors. They might be friends or family at first, then banks or other entrepreneurs. They'll probably want shares in your business in return for their money. Investors may also give you good advice. Listen carefully and change your business idea if necessary.

⑤ TELL EVERYONE

Having a good business idea is important. But telling people about it is even more important. No one will use your business if they don't know about it. Sometimes it's helpful to pay for adverts, but often the best advertising is free. Ask your friends to tell their friends to tell their friends (Facebook and Twitter are good for this)! Think of ways to get your business into newspapers, blogs and TV and radio shows too.

LIKE | COMMENT | ✉   posted by GemDesign

⑥ KEEP MOVING FORWARD

Is your business successful? That's fantastic! But remember, the world changes fast. This year's most exciting website might be old and boring next year. Keep thinking about new and exciting ideas for your business if you want your success to continue.

Good luck!

> Work in pairs. Do you have an idea for a new business? What is it?

> **What do these words mean? You can use a dictionary.**
> research   risk / risky   investor   advertising   blog

CHAPTERS 1–2

Before you read

You can use your dictionary for these questions.

1 Use these words to complete the sentences.

adopt   animated   case   create   digital
expert   junkyard   keyboard

a) I found an old car door at the _____ .

b) They couldn't have children, so they decided to _____ a baby.

c) Use the _____ to type your name.

d) I love _____ films like *Shrek*.

e) He's an _____ in computer programming.

f) I keep my glasses in the _____ when I'm not wearing them.

g) The _____ camera was invented in 1975.

h) I want to _____ a machine that will make the world a better place.

2 Answer the questions.

a) Which **arts** subjects do / did you learn at school?

b) Are there any factories in your area? What **products** do they make?

c) What are the most important **industries** in your country?

d) Name some successful **entrepreneurs** from your country. What businesses did they start?

e) Who are the most **powerful** people in your country?

After you read

3 Match the places and companies with the sentences.

Atari   India   Hewlett-Packard   Oregon   Syria

a) Steve's birth father came from here.

b) Steve went to a computer club here.

c) Steve went to university here.

d) Steve worked here after university.

e) Steve travelled here to find out more about religion.

4 Why were these people important in Steve's life?

a) Joanne Schieble   b) Paul Jobs   c) Larry Lang
d) Daniel Kottke   e) Steve Wozniak   f) Paul Terrell

CHAPTERS 3–6

Before you read

5 Match the words with the descriptions.

advert   determined   genius   operating system
public   shares

a) This is the software in a computer that helps all the programs to work together.

b) This adjective describes a person who never stops trying.

c) People who own a company have these.

d) A company uses this to tell you about a product that they want you to buy.

e) This is the opposite of *private*.

f) This is unusually high intelligence or skill.

6 The title of Chapter 5 is 'Starting again'. Why did Steve have to start again, do you think?

After you read

7 Match the two halves of the sentences.

a) The Apple II   i) was Steve's company after he left Apple.

b) The Lisa   ii) had an innovative operating system but was too slow.

c) Xerox   iii) gave Steve some exciting ideas for computers.

d) The Macintosh   iv) was a project which Steve wasn't allowed to finish.

e) NeXT   v) was a very popular computer.

8 Choose the correct word.

a) *Mike Markkula / John Sculley* taught Steve a lot about business.

b) Steve *was / wasn't* a very good father to Lisa when she was a young child.

c) The Macintosh advert *was / wasn't* very successful.

d) The NeXT computers were for *universities / films*.

e) Steve met his *birth mother / birth father* and his sister.

f) Steve had four *wives / children*.

CHAPTERS 7-10

Before you read

9 Guess the answers to these questions. Then read and check.
   a) Steve returned to work at Apple. Why?
   b) Was his management style different from when he worked there before? In what ways?
   c) What important new products did he help to create?
   d) Steve spent a long time in hospital. Why?

After you read

10 Put these sentences in the correct order.
    a) Apple started selling the iPod.
    b) Steve sold Pixar to Disney.
    c) Steve sold NeXT to Apple.
    d) Steve found out that he had cancer.
    e) Steve decided to help the music industry.
    f) Tim Cook became CEO of Apple.
    g) The iPhone went on sale.

11 Are these sentences true or false? Correct the false sentences.
    a) A lot of people lost their jobs when Steve returned to Apple.
    b) Steve suggested the unusual shape of the first iMac.
    c) The first iPod was more expensive than other MP3 players.
    d) Steve had an operation for his cancer as soon as possible.
    e) The glass in the iPhone was a new invention.
    f) The iPad was very popular.
    g) The Beatles were the first musicians to have their music on iTunes.
    h) Steve designed a new boat before he died.

12 What do you think? Answer these questions.
    a) Which of Apple's products has brought the biggest changes?
    b) Was Apple a good place to work when Steve was CEO? Why / Why not?
    c) In your opinion, what was Steve Jobs' greatest achievement?